THE UNTOLD STORY OF A. E. MCRAE

Life Matters of the Heart

The Untold Story

By:

A. E. McRae

LIFE MATTERS OF THE HEART

BlaqRayn Publishing
134 Andrew Drive
Reidsville, North Carolina 27320

****

Printed in the United States of America

ISBN: 9798700850278

Published by: **BlaqRayn Publishing** 2021
Printed by: **Kindle Direct Publishing** 2021

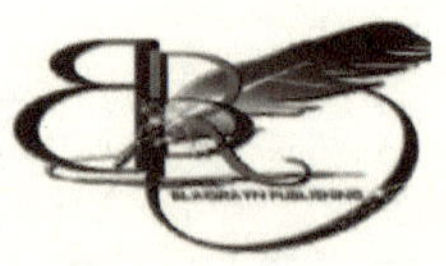

Dedication

I dedicate this, my first published work of poetry, to Myself.

~A. E. McRae

THE UNTOLD STORY OF A. E. MCRAE

Life Matters of the Heart

The Untold Story

A.E. McRae

Introduction

With my words, I will take
you on a journey through
my deepest emotions.
Giving you moments filled
with whirlwinds and
escapades of my heart's
composition.

As you see the world being
revealed through my eyes,
you get to walk through
my physical trials as they
uncover my spiritual birth.

Why I Write

When the pathway to my audible doesn't
seem to find its destination to my mouth
I find consolation within the stroke of
the pen to the pad.

Words overload my brain like a cosmic
atmosphere filled with the explosions
made against the sky during the 4th of
July.

I write to show the emotions that one
may feel. Like the things that we go
through that must allow us to heal.

It is in this that I have discovered the
power of relation without experiencing
the physicality of it. Drawing forth what
some may never find understanding in.
As I bring life to a meaning sometimes
well hidden when it's still.

But most importantly, I write because it is an extension of a gift granted by the one who has announced himself as the Most High.

Inspiration

Strong men never seem to forget about
the weakness in their brother.

A weakness that comes to bring
discouragement in their time of distress.

A realization that his aid may not always
come from those who wear familiar faces.

So as the rain drenched among the Sierra
Desert he provides encouragement to
replenish the dry soul.

Reaching into the depth of his heart so
that he may pull out the nutrients of
success that enable another to say I won't
give up.

No Matter What

How is it that you love me despite all the
things I have done?

When I only loved myself enough to
think love was between the crevices that
aligned my legs.

When I readily embraced the one who
wanted death to the description above
my head.

Through all of this you

the consistent one

declared your love as more than being
words said.

As I lied to those who trust me carried
my name

I pondered on the thought of

won't you fear

that to you I will do the same?

But in the discretion of a gentle humility

you comforted me in your assurance.

And as tears rolled down my face and I fell to my knees, you reached out your hand to me saying

"no matter what I'll always love you."

Because Of You

I live because you decided to give
your breathe for mine. Each of your
marked stripes have healed me from
my worst illness.

Grace came to restore

While favor opened many doors.

Your voice detoured me from taking
a dangerous path which led me to the
understanding of why obedience is
learned and life is the saturation of
blessings earned.

Just One Tear

A tear takes on a downward position
against my face.

Your hand

it acts as a glove catching it before it
becomes destroyed by life's floor.

Bursting in your palm emerging
scenes from my life.

I smile but yet I cry out in
undeniable pain.

I offer happiness to everyone but the
one who stares at me in the mirror.

I live but inside I am dying.

I am strong as steel but as weak a child.

Asleep in darkness but through Christ I have awakened.

The Water

***It seeps between your fingers,
closing a wound that once was
wide open.***

***And as I look into your eyes, I
realize, every thought that once
was a question you have just
given an answer.***

***Exposing the truth as to why life
is the product of undeniable
Grace.***

With You

Becoming what you want me to be is my most sought after desire.

You have graced me with your presence, allowing me to experience a greater part of life. Every step I take I want to be guided by you.

Your word

the foundation of my life molds me like the potter and his clay. Never will I worry about facing my greatest fears alone.

With you

The one who remains by my side,

my fears turn themselves into triumphs.

My **Alpha**

My **Omega**

you have become.

Making my body, soul, and spirit submit
to you as one.

Your eyes

They show me a light that I could never
ignore.

Your love

It defies the law of all that is ordinary

which has convinced me that my
decision to be like you is one that will
forever be considered extraordinary.

No More Excuses

I thought I knew victory

but I never accomplished anything.

I said I was a witness

but I never gave my testimony.

I tried to be a leader

but could never figure out how to follow.

I gave man my word

but never gave him honor.

I wanted to change my life

but there were still some things I had to do.

I wanted to stop making excuses

but then the question would remain who are you?

Life's Questions

How can you justify the feeling of insecurity when it comes from within?

Does not knowing hurt worst than knowing?

If truth was the revelation of your subconscious would you know the manner in which one was awake?

Is change only effective when it happens to you?

Life in itself is a question but true revaluation is the work that is completed to find the journey's answer.

Help Me (1)

When the perplexity of a situation isn't consistent with the direction of my faith's vertical stance, will you be there?

To accomplish the things that I can no longer do by myself.

In the execution of having things done my way, the recognition that I must depend upon you

The one who composed me from skin to bone.

A part of me consumed with fear

Feels you may not understand the delivery in my message because the urgency of my cry resembles the footprints of more than desperation.

My only hope is that you will find me and place your guidance upon these feet so that they lose the sound that has become the cousin child of hope mixed with frustration.

Thank You

Just when I was about to give up

my soul became infused with your hope.

Life without you was not birthed like
an endless whirlwind and the creation
of time was made evident in the
victories that came because of you.

Your Grace

Gave immense ability to endure the hell
submerged in my trial and tribulations.

So for that I thank you for the liberty in
what is now my life.

My Life

I took a breath of life for the first time and knew I was myself.

Gazing into the eyes of another, I concluded that they were the compilation of another.

I took my first steps not knowing where to go.

Said my first words not knowing what to say.

But the moment I took one look at you I knew you were love.

Still I Love You

Because of you I am hurting.

My heart has been dipped in the liquid of
your pain. I have let you pour your acid
of hurt into my life but still I love you.

My tears

they form a river of their own but still I
love you.

I remember the days when the picture
painted seem to be good but somehow

it became overshadowed by rips tattooed
in the canvas.

Through your countenance is a truth
covered by lies, but still I love you.

Is my pain not recognizable through my
distant smile?

At times it seemed easier to love you than to love myself. Not once did I choose to love someone's heart while loving yours but the visibility of that is not in this pain that I carry.

My greatest fear has produced drifts of me losing you not just to someone else but losing you completely. I allowed my spirit to become magnetically drawn to you as I release my soul to you.

Not realizing that you could never fully complete the inner parts of me because you didn't desire to be apart of what heals me.

Letting your mistakes become my mistakes as I made space to still be the one who chose to love you…

Together

Our time together has proven to be more than a vain imprint in time but a preparation of God's plan.

God has shown me the key to winning your heart is in him. All the pain and heartache has been turned into endless happiness.

Two wrongs didn't make it right but one right changed it all. You unveiled me, making us one.

Changing every path so that we would be a design that pleased God.

I have learned to love you as I love myself, that's why our unity has such a sacred bond.

We overcame the tests and trials that were thrown in our direction, linking our past and present to distinguish our future.

We Use To

We use to spend nights looking into the stars, gazing into each other's eyes but the way the sun sets looks different now.

Love

It was the mesmerizing effect of our presence when we were together.

Rainy days took on the appearance of a body's amiable physics creating the personal story lines in a romantic best seller.

Things once considered most important have found their way in an unforgotten state.

Causing my need for you to be like a conviction to a plant without water.

My want for you is as passionate as the fire
that burns between two lovers.

We used to be so tight that nobody could
come between us.

I never wanted us to be each other's
shadow because that just wasn't my style.

There is a nonexistence of the things that
we use to do

But change and time came into our lives
and now we are here

Stuck pondering on the memory of what
we used to be.

You're Losing Me Baby

I never thought the day would come
when I wanted to say goodbye.

You gave me a love of what I perceived
to be unconditional for quite some time
now.

To love you and leave you without
saying why

came from the moments produced when
my heart knew the truth even when I
tried to change it.

Rest never allowed me to call upon its
name until I had the courage to do what
was needed.

Don't think I didn't love you but the
inspiration to love me more came into
existence.

And I fell immensely in love with her.

The one who waited to show me that she
loved me the most.

I Hate You

You came into my life carrying the
infantry of so much stress.

You never took the time to see that with
me you were blessed.

In my anger and rage, I would destroy
your most prized possession

Hoping you would change and learn a
lesson.

Every chance I get I'll make your life a
living hell and be on my merry way,
content and well.

I could easily end your life right now

But I want you to suffer the breaths and
actions of your how.

My mind plays the tape of deceitfulness
so there's no wonder my heart no longer
has love

And is filled with the hollowness of a
cold emptiness.

I Love You

My heart ..

It finds a way to skip to the rhythm
of love's drum even when your
physical being is not around.

In your arms, I feel like a delicate
rose blossoming from the ground.

An eternal future with you is what I
see when your eyes are locked with
mine

Enduring hardships and triumphing
over many victories.

Causing the soul of me to take abode
in you.

Giving you the reason within my life

to be the warrior in my distress

The comforter when I need rest.

A declaration to the world that you
are my diamond produced from a
pearl.

Someone Else

It's hard to look at you and see you with
her.

I ponder on the mere thought of do you
think of me when you're with her.

Does the passion in your kiss with her
resemble the one that we share?

Does the thought of me being the one
you're holding at night ever come to you
in your dreams?

When I'm with you do you ever think
about she's doing?

Having you in my presence

I picture it being a world filled with only
the two of us.

The luminous light that you have placed upon my face is the replacement of a thousand candle lights.

Often times my feelings for you have made me forget how dangerous it is that you and I belong to someone else.

What A Woman Wants

Uplift my spirit so that peace is the
reason we exist.

When you look at me show me that
it's me and only me who you love.

Protect me from the dangers that
come to lay traces of evil.

Console me.

When I am hurt

pay attention to how it speaks.

So I don't build a wall against you.

Trust me so that I may trust you.

Help me to understand you so that
you can understand me.

Because really all this woman wants
is the security in the one who holds
her heart.

Emotions

I've felt pain but does anyone care?

I've cried a stream of endless tears so
long that I have forgot how to stop them.

Can I ever make myself happy if I am
always trying to make another smile but
does anyone care?

Take a look in the mirror and tell me
what you see.

Is it something worth seeing or someone
you can't stand to be?

What can I do to enhance the person
that's looking back at me?

Not knowing where to begin when I've
forgotten how to find the end.

Leading life to spin in circles like
destructive whirlwinds

Gathering chaos in the midst, as it takes
me by destructive force.

Imprinting a hole in the place where
footsteps should have been.

Anger

Pushes me like a pierced knife to the soul.

It crawls up inside me making me its
habitat in a dark hole.

The stronger it gets, the more I suppress
it

To keep the sanity that lies within me.

It ticks me like a time bomb ready to
blow up, leading to nothing but self
destruction.

I asked myself

How can I be the one to give
encouragement when it's needed for
myself?

Expectations of a presentation to smile lie
dormant

As my heart wears a frown carried by a massive weight.

It's like a conversation that contains issues once left alone when really they were made for a round table discussion.

The commitment of the grass being greener on the other side is like that of a false doctrine.

Actions received on the outre will be spent holding on to emotions painted by the course of things that lead to nothing.

Causing the roots of everything displayed to be creation of an anger turned evil.

The Fork In Your Life

As you come to the fork in the road,
making a conscious decision on what
your future will bring shatters you.

Should you go to the left?

Staying on the path of no change, only to
experience what is familiar to you?

Letting your life remain stuck in an
unawareness you are continuously
blinded by situations because you can't
bring yourself to see the other side.

The fact that growth and development
are buried under frozen ground leads
your feet to be trapped in yesterday.

Questioning every step made with
audible reasons of should've, could've,
but didn't.

Glares possessed through the right side
create scenes of your future.

And as they glance back at you

statements of wonder are birthed as you
are left pondering if you have the guts to
take the first step.

The fear of what must remain behind in
your life showers you with emotions.

Overlapping moments of discretion with
an anxiety of the unknown.

To stay looking at both sides of the fork

not ever making a decision

you'll never crossed the door of
opportunity.

Someone Take Me Away

Things occur to perpetuate the feeling
of going away forever.

The harder I try to fix things the deeper
the mess seems to get.

The odds of getting through the tunnel
without having to struggle is like
walking through the life's darkness
without light.

I never thought the day would come
when I would be down and there was
no one around.

My worst fear is not being able to
depend on myself

Now it stares me in the face

Paralyzed with distress

What do I do?

Who do I turn to?

When the reality hits that there is no one to take me away.

Who's Watching Me

Your eyes look at me in a mundane
way

Not knowing the complexity of my
being.

Life

Not giving you your signal to detour
on the next stop.

As sly as a fox you pass me not
realizing that

I the hawk quietly sit back and
observe your every move.

Your robust actions keep me puzzled
about what you will perform next.

You

as sly as a fox continue to deceive
while

I the hawk sit back quietly and
observe you be the watchman of me.

Changes of The Future

If the future was me what would it be?

Would things be changed to
accommodate the present state of it all
or would I succumb to the changes of
how it should be?

Facing the truth seems harder to
manifest when it is seen

And the reality of it hits harder because
it must be confronted.

If seeing the future forces one to change

What is the depth of it being called a
reality that doesn't remain the same?

Tomorrow

Look at tomorrow as an opportunity
missed by yesterday

and a day hoped to be seized by you.

If yesterday is just looked at as being
yesterday

Then you'll never understand why
tomorrow has to come.

And the crack in the door of
tomorrow can't be opened

Blocking the fulfillment of your
dreams with an irreversible damage.

Rain

Rain falls hard when no one is listening

Keeping a steady steam no matter whether you're sleep or awake

It still falls with the intent to make things wet.

Just as life is given, it is also taken

And as the air fills the sky you become aware of how important life must be.

Is it right to think wrong or is working to always be right a set up to experience a flood?

Do you value time more when you have it or when it is gone? Is the change of the seasons more important when there is no rain?

The answers to these questions deserve the water of truth instead of the death that comes when one is trapped in the desert.

Water In My Heart

The agony of knowing you're not
here makes me sorrowful.

I tried to forget about what it was
doing to me.

However vivid scenes took over my
mental causing what I wanted to let
go become what I remembered.

Although reality made it hard to
visualize you any other way.

Still I took you for granted

And as the recollections of you
resurfaced

The water is my heart became the
tears I know no more.

Memories

Memories invade my mind like a
mighty warrior in battle.

Good ones,

Bad ones,

Happy ones,

Sorrowful ones.

They embrace curves taken when
traveling short term escapades that
dance from side to side like ball
players on game day.

Long term journeys leave tracks that
can never be erased.

Giving sound to time's rapidly
beating drum never slowing down or

missing a beat to the prediction of
the universe's heat.

What Is Why?

Why doesn't always produce an answer, making it harder to become as one believes.

Believing

Is the catalyst to what makes us become whatever it is that we have been perceived to be.

Thoughts

Words

Actions

One must take the stage as the most powerful when life answers to the curtain call.

Scene one....the thought forms it's existence

Scene two... the words they labor the floorboards of the stage

Scene three....actions announce themselves as the encore to it all.

The application of what is the underground motive of the thought takes a bow.

Allowing the process to be the chain that links it all.

With the understanding that thought may not be concluded with a definite answer.

Unspoken Words

My eyes

They tell what my lips cannot reveal.

My heart

shows emotions with intensity?

My mind

noting words but to the audible tone
there is no utterance.

My mirror can no longer hide behind the
shade of fog

While my spirit man wants to leap out.

After the tears stop the feelings subjected
to subside will remain at attention.

Cries in the light of darkness allow me to
be heard..

Dazed

My eyes need the comfort of someone whose reassurance is given in the simple things.

I can never give my part if I am always made to give more.

The most dangerous thing that a person could do is to allow their mind to wonder while letting commitment scare them from what's really in the heart.

Creating a dialogue of unspoken words in a conversation afraid to be held.

Undeniable

It's hard for you to accept the truth
when you hold on to the past.

You hurt because you allow yourself
to love without eyes.

Your strength is blanketed by your
weaknesses.

Tomorrow can never embrace you if
continue to dwell on yesterday as if it
were an uncharted weight.

It's easier for you to say you can't
while all along you're just frighten by
the fact that you can.

To completely live you must live in
the truth that your life is better when

You acknowledge that it belongs to the one who has given you the ability to live.

Help Me (2)

Help!

Someone is chasing me!

I look to the left,

To the right

And it's their face I see.

Behind a rock I stand

and there they stand also.

I take solace in the darkest corner and they stand beside me.

I am tired of running from them so I stop and turn around to unmask this mysterious person

But nobody's there because the person I'm running from is me.

My Unborn Child

I'm sorry I didn't love myself enough
to hear your cry to live.

I never gave you the chance to look
into my eyes and call me mommy.

Your smile never got the chance to be
the light for another.

You didn't get to hear me whisper to
you how much I love you

Or experience the comfort of my
embrace.

Your desire to live is expressed
through the pain that stabs my heart
daily.

I hear your cries and laughter and
regret that those are the sounds of my
unborn child.

Not Just An Ordinary Day

(A prayer)

Today I am asking for something more than the average. Let your face show through me in a way that causes situations to change because I speak them.

Allow love to touch the heart that is molded by stone. Close the wounds of the one that is hurt and lonely.

Shelter the man that has lost his home and open his eyes and ears so that your glorious work may be known.

Raising A Man

(A Declaration)

As a baby, my son can't defend for himself.

His determination of what is good and bad is the reflection of me.

The growth from a boy to a man must possess the installation of being truthful not just to his self observation but to others.

When it seems easier for him to involve himself in fraudulence he must realize the effect that it will have on the person of the receiving end.

Establishing a reaction that could turn out to be deadly or tear a person apart.

Stepping into the transition of a man
the responsibilities that come with
being a man shall be executed with
maturity.

Sacrifices are just part of the painted
picture.

In the expression of his veridical
emotions, his strength should not be
comprised.

Most importantly truth must always put
its foot forward.

So that his interpretation of respect is
not just a given but it is one that is
earned.

And he takes value in my contribution
in raising him to be a man.

About the Author

Born to the name of Amendrius McRae, I was given life on November 19, 1980 by Emma and Ricky McRae.

Growing up, I experienced the typical middle class childhood. Both my parents were hard working people and taught me the value of working for what I wanted to have out of life.

My love for writing has been with me since my early years as well as being a lover of the arts. I have a background in Early Childhood Education and have had the privilege of working as a preschool teacher for over 20 years.

"**Life Matters of the Heart**" is my first published work of poetry but it certainly will not be my last.

Author A. E. McRae

www.ingramcontent.com/pod-product-compliance
Lightning Source LLC
LaVergne TN
LVHW091229150826
845673LV00003B/1072

* 9 7 9 8 7 0 0 8 5 0 2 7 8 *